Liam's Story

So why do I wear Dad's medals?

Marg Baber — University of New England

Madeline Fussell — University of New England

Kim Porter — University of New England

Edited by Susan Feez — University of New England

Pademelon Press

First published 2015 by Pademelon Press
PO Box 42, Mt Victoria NSW 2786
www.pademelonpress.com.au

Creator:	Baber, Marg, author.
Title:	Liam's story : so why do I wear dad's medals? / Marg Baber, Madeline Fussell, Kim Porter.
ISBN:	9781876138431 (paperback)
Notes:	Includes bibliographical references.
Target Audience:	For primary school age.
Subjects:	1. World War, 1914-1918—Medals—Juvenile literature. 2. World War, 1914-1918—Campaigns—Turkey—Gallipoli 3. Peninsula—Juvenile literature. 4. Anzac Day—Juvenile literature.
Other Creators/Contributors:	Fussell, Madeline, author. Porter, Kim Anne, author.

Dewey Number: 940.426

Editor: Susan Feez
Project Manager and Editor: Madeline Fussell
Includes links to download extension activities and teaching programs for parents and teachers written by Madeline Fussell, Kim Porter, Susan Feez and edited by Marg Baber
Printed by Ligare Book Printers

The paper this publication is printed on is certified by the Forest Stewardship Council (FSC) ®1996 FSC A.C. The FSC promotes environmentally responsible, socially beneficial and economically viable management of the world's forests.

The staff of Pademelon Press live and work on the land of the Tharawal and Wiradjuri peoples. The authors work at the University of New England, the traditional home of the Anaiwan people in the ancestral land of the Ngawanya. We acknowledge and respect the Traditional Owners and Custodians of these lands and pay our respects to the Elders past, present and future.

About this book

This book is the first in a series to be published in relation to research about the experiences of military families being undertaken by researchers at the University of New England, NSW. This research was initially prompted when Madeline Fussell, a Primary Social Science Lecturer, was approached by military families who expressed their frustration at the lack of culturally authentic and age-appropriate illustrated storybooks for their young children. They asked for books that supported the experiences of young children who had a parent deploying or absent for extended periods during training. They identified common related issues encountered by military families. Teaming up with Marg Baber, an Early Childhood Lecturer, they met with two military families and discussed some of these issues. This resulted in several research-based illustrated storybooks being written as a community project for the charity organisation, Soldier On. Further background research revealed there was almost no Australian and little international research working directly with young children to explore their experiences and understandings of their lives in military families; nor was there research that allowed young military children's voices to be heard. Marg's research aims to address this gap. Her doctoral thesis is titled 'Young children's experiences and understanding of military deployment within an Australian Defence Force family'. This study has resulted in the production of many storybooks that were employed throughout the research phase with children from military families. Families and educators have also used these storybooks and found them very helpful as a starting point to discuss a diverse range of issues, including:

- military deployment or training
- any child's experience when their parent works away
- an injured parent and
- a parent with Post Traumatic Stress Disorder and other mental health issues.

This publication also incorporates the research of Madeline Fussell and Kim Porter in the area of Social Science Primary Teaching. The concepts in this book will be augmented in a forthcoming book explaining the significance of Remembrance Day.

For extension activities and teaching programs suitable for parents and teachers that have been written by Madeline Fussell, Kim Porter and Susan Feez and edited by Marg Baber, please go to www.pademelonpress.com.au and search for the page for Liam's Story.

Foreword by Barry J Clark

BJ Clark QSM

The Royal New Zealand Returned and Services Association, often referred to as the **Returned Services Association** but best known simply as the RSA, is one of the largest voluntary welfare organisations in New Zealand. It is also one of the oldest ex-service organisations in the world.

The RSA's commitment to veterans' welfare is embodied in Poppy Day when red poppies are exchanged for donations and hundreds of thousands of New Zealanders raise funds for the welfare of all veterans and in remembrance of New Zealand's war dead.

As with our Australian comrades, our current veterans are facing many of the same issues that our predecessors did, but we now have better resources and supports. There is also an increased awareness of the effects service has on our defence personnel.

On reading *Liam's story: So why do I wear Dad's medals?*, I am reminded that not only are service personnel affected by their service but so too are our families. This book asks the question that too many children have had to ask or who perhaps never found the words to ask. Today we are seeing a significant increase in the younger generation attending ANZAC Day; they have questions and expect honest answers.

I am pleased to support this publication and I am sure that all who read it will relate to the questions Liam asks and the difficulties faced by parents in these situations. The multi-level nature of the book ensures it is a prized resource for all.

We have a duty to ensure that the families affected by service receive the support they require.

Lest We Forget

BJ Clark QSM JP
RSA National President

Foreword by Don Rowe OAM

Don Rowe, OAM

The Returned and Services League (RSL) was formed in 1917 to support both serving and ex-service Australian Defence Force (ADF) personnel and their families. Over the years, the problems faced by ADF veterans, and their families, have largely remained the same, but in that time our knowledge about and treatment of these problems has improved enormously.

The commemoration of ANZAC Day is an important date on the calendar in both Australia and New Zealand. Whilst it is hoped that this day serves to teach about our history and to remind us all of the price paid by so many of our ADF personnel for the many freedoms we enjoy, it also reminds us that there are many in our communities today who have been affected by the horrors of war, and who need our understanding and assistance.

There are very few soldiers who return from active service who are not changed in some way. As a means of assisting veterans to reintegrate into civilian life and of ensuring recognition of the unique and ongoing sacrifice of veterans' families, the value of community understanding cannot be overstated.

This book has my enthusiastic support as I have witnessed on both a professional and personal basis the daily struggle that so many face as a result of war. It is my hope that this book will not only generate knowledge about and understanding of the ANZAC Day commemoration but will also build awareness of those in our communities who, because of their experience of war, need our continued understanding and assistance. There can be no better way to honour our fallen than by supporting those whom they loved.

Don Rowe

State President of The Returned and Services League of Australia (New South Wales Branch) from November 2003–November 2014
Elected Deputy National President September 2005–2014

Foreword by David Gray

David Gray

Legacy is as relevant today as it was following the Great War of 2014–2018.

The first Legacy Club was started in Melbourne in 1923 by Lieutenant-General (later Sir) Stan Savige and since then Legacy has provided care and support to many hundreds of thousands of family members of those soldiers, sailors and airmen and women who have given their lives or health in the defence of Australia. Today, after 90+ years of service by Legacy volunteers, Legacy still cares for around 90 000 family members ranging in age from four months to 109 years and the task is not going away in the foreseeable future.

Legacy stands ready to bring its core ethos of Mateship, Personal Service and Service to Children to the commemoration of the birth of ANZAC at Gallipoli and the important realisation and acknowledgement of the impact of all conflicts on families and the sacrifices they have made and continue to make in the protection of our country and the values we hold dear.

This book is a family focused recognition of those sacrifices brought to realisation in this centenary year in a respectful, factual and informative style to assist the important educational needs of our younger generation. This is in keeping with the Legacy ethos and we support this worthwhile initiative.

David Gray
Chairman, Legacy Australia Incorporated

Reading and using this book

This illustrated story book has been designed to be read on three levels. The yellow banner at the top of each page can be read by itself to the youngest audience. The combination of the banner and the larger print below it carries the story and is for slightly older children and should be read through first. The whole text provides information for an older audience. Children will seek to learn more with each reading as adults scaffold their learning to the next level. This true story provides an initial understanding of ANZAC Day and a good stimulus, at any level, for parents, educators and family workers. The book can be used in conjunction with the downloadable extension activities and teaching notes to meet curriculum requirements.
Please go to www.pademelonpress.com.au and search for the page for Liam's Story.

Words that appear in **bold** type are defined in the Glossary on page 38.

Memorial of Turkish soldier rescuing an Allied forces captain at Pine Ridge, Gallipoli

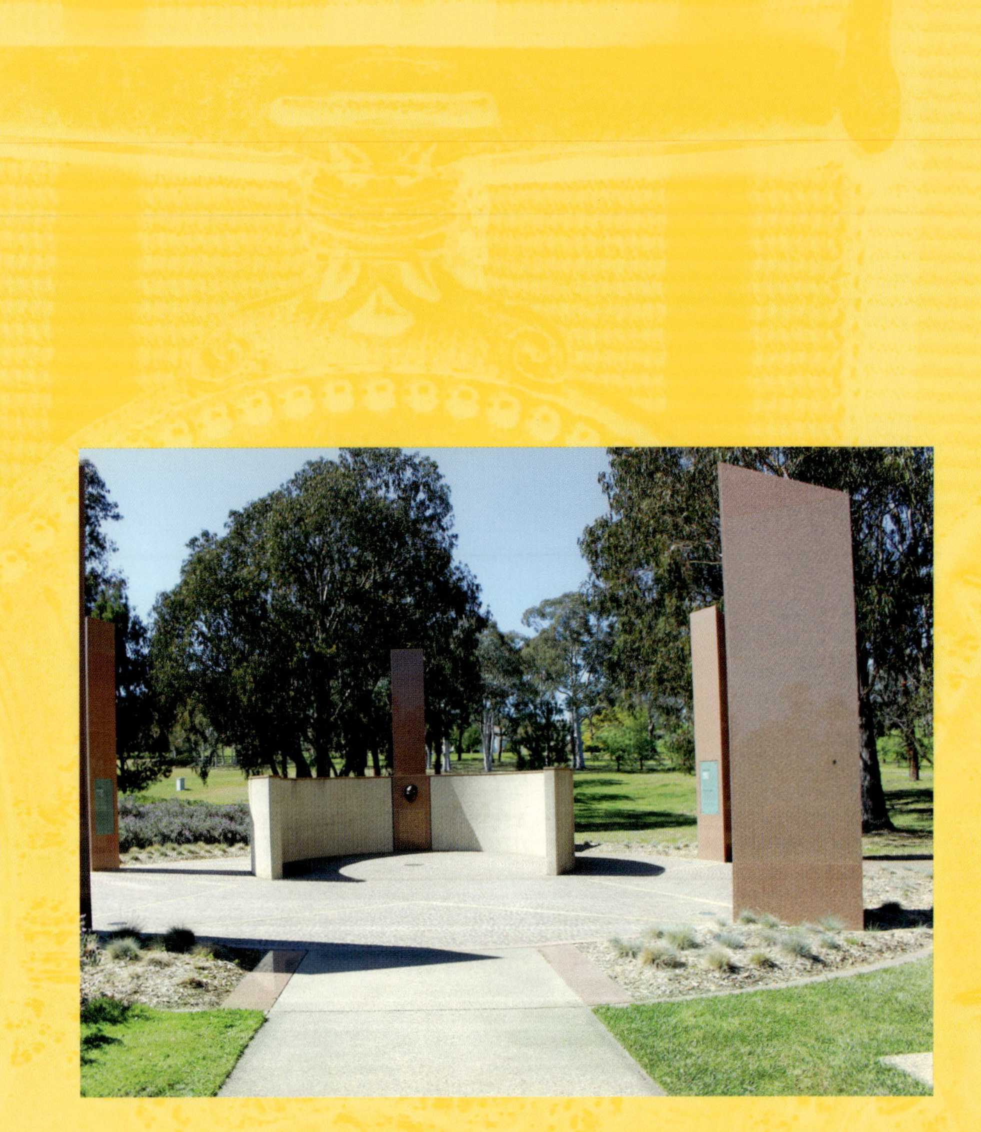

Australian memorial to Kemal Atatürk, Canberra

Liam's story

This book originated through a telephone conversation with a distressed mother seeking guidance to answer the question asked by her five-year-old about why he wears his Dad's medals on ANZAC Day. This mother suggested that there had to be a better answer than 'Daddy died' ... and of course there is. There is a rich and complex answer involving global, national, community and personal perspectives that results in the wearing of such medals. This book is Liam's explanation, and one that we hope will bring understanding to the people he encounters and many more.

Teaching about ANZAC Day, and other significant commemorations in Australia and New Zealand is important. It is a dedicated part of the Australian Curriculum: History K–12 (2012) and the New Zealand Social Science curriculum for primary students. Approaching such subject matter with young children can be difficult. If treated with too much detail and honesty, children will be traumatised; treated superficially, we risk glorifying war and perpetuating myths and legends. The objective of this book is to explain the truth and the traditions of this day. Young children, like adults, can understand if they can empathise. This story gives honest insight into what it means to be a five-year-old Legacy child. It also provides additional information on the traditions and rituals that have built up in both Australia and New Zealand around this now very nationalistic day.

Liam's story: So why do I wear Dad's medals?, provides conversation starters and stimulus for further learning as children are introduced to the commemoration of those who have died through conflicts. They also learn to understand some of the effects this has on families, communities and nations. History contains great achievements, tragic situations and consequences. We need to learn from each of these and contribute to change as best we can. Children, like us all, cope better if they can see some productive action is taken. This book clearly shows that soldiers and their families are very much part of the communities we live in and often need our support and that there is something we can do.

Pseudonyms have been used in this book to protect the privacy of some individuals.

Here's what some other children said about *Liam's Story.*

I liked the way he was really young, but he still got up early and did all that stuff. I also liked the way he tried to remember his dad. The last reason why I like it is because he was brave and he thought how proud his dad would be of him for wearing his medals.
Eevi, 7 years

I thought it was great and I liked he had to wear the medals to show people.
Huon, 5 years

Each year on ANZAC Day,

the 25th of April,
my day is completely different
from every other day.

On this day, a long time ago, soldiers landed at a small beach at Gallipoli, an area in Turkey. These soldiers were from Australia and New Zealand. ANZAC is an acronym for Australia and New Zealand Army Corp. Most of these soldiers were volunteers. For nine long months they fought and lived in atrocious conditions. The ANZACs and allied forces were the invaders in Turkey and were defeated at Gallipoli by the Turkish Army. The campaign is recognised as a disaster that resulted in huge loss of life and injuries for both sides. It was the first time for Australia, as a nation, to be involved in a war. Today we call this beach ANZAC Cove and soldiers are remembered for the courage, mateship and perseverance they displayed there.

Why do you think we commemorate the Gallipoli campaign when it was not successful?

April

Mon	Tue	Wed	Thur	Fri	Sat	Sun
30	31	1	2	3	4	5
6	7	8	9	10	11	12
13	14	15	16	17	18	19
20	21	22	23	24	25	26
27	28	29	30	1	2	3

Turkish tour guide showing a drawing of the Anzac Cove landing in 1915

ANZAC Cove today, Gallipoli, Turkey

Mum wakes me early, **seriously early,**

to go to the dawn service in the dark. She irons my clothes and lays them on my bed with Dad's medals and a metal wrist band with his name engraved on it.

The men sailed to Gallipoli in Turkey on big ships. At dawn, little boats were lowered over the side of the ships and the men rowed to the tiny beach. As they tried to land, many were killed or injured. Those who made it ashore had to stay alive with very basic **rations**, not enough water and constant danger.

This is why there is a 'Dawn Service' held on ANZAC Day. Later in the morning there is a march and another service in many places big and small.

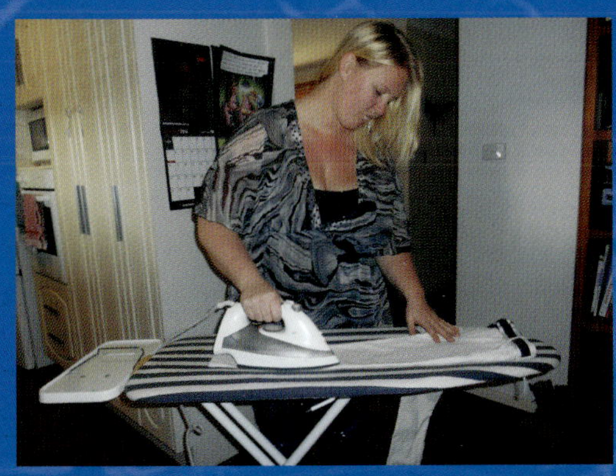

She says I have to look my best ...

as everyone will be there.
We need to show our respect to all those who have served in wars.

People in small towns and big cities, all over Australia and New Zealand, come together to commemorate ANZAC Day. Within ten years of the end of World War One (1914–1918), most towns and cities in Australia and New Zealand had built **memorials** and posted **rolls of honour**. In both Australia and New Zealand, 25th April is a **public holiday** and most shops and businesses are shut until after the **morning services** and the **marches**.

World War Two veteran with her son wearing his father's medals

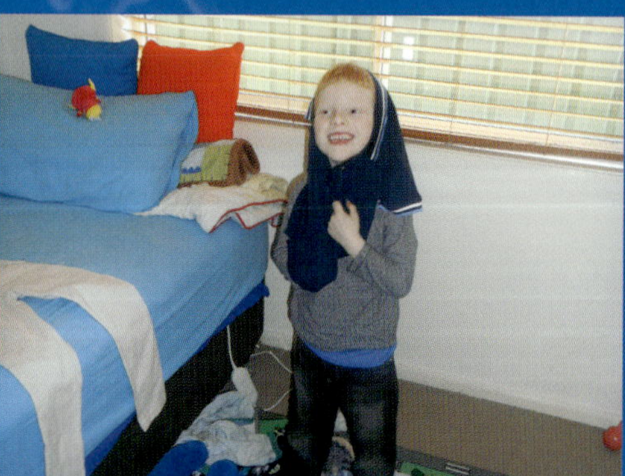

So tell me, why do I wear Dad's medals?

Here are the medals Liam wears. On which side would he wear them?

Why do you think Liam wears his father's medals?

Medals in Australia are worn on the left at chest height. Medals are worn on the right side if they are worn by a relative.

Medals are awarded for active service. This means the person has worked in a **war zone**. They may have been a medical officer, a mechanic, a pilot — there are lots of different jobs that need to be done. The **campaign** medal tells where the service was. There is a medal for peacekeeping service and for non-warlike service too. There are **gallantry** medals to honour outstanding achievements.

The guards surround the monument,

a lone piper plays, speeches are made,
a song is sung, the bugle plays
and the ode is read.

At the end of the day, a piece called the 'Last Post' was traditionally played on the **bugle** to signify the end of the day for the troops. At ANZAC Day services it is played on a bugle, cornet or trumpet to signify that those who have died can now rest in peace. After the 'Last Post' is played, everyone is silent for one minute to show their respect and gratitude to all who have died as a result of military service.

A **Catafalque Party** is the special military guard of four uniformed people who guard the monument as they would guard the **coffin** of a fallen comrade.

My Dad's name is read out ...

and Mum blows her nose.
After the service, journalists take photos and many others do too.

Since the end of World War Two, many **service men and women** have been involved in **peacekeeping** missions, **surveillance** and **border protection** in different parts of the world. This often means they witness **tragedy.** People in some countries have been **traumatically** affected by conflict in their country. On ANZAC Day we remember these **service personnel** too.

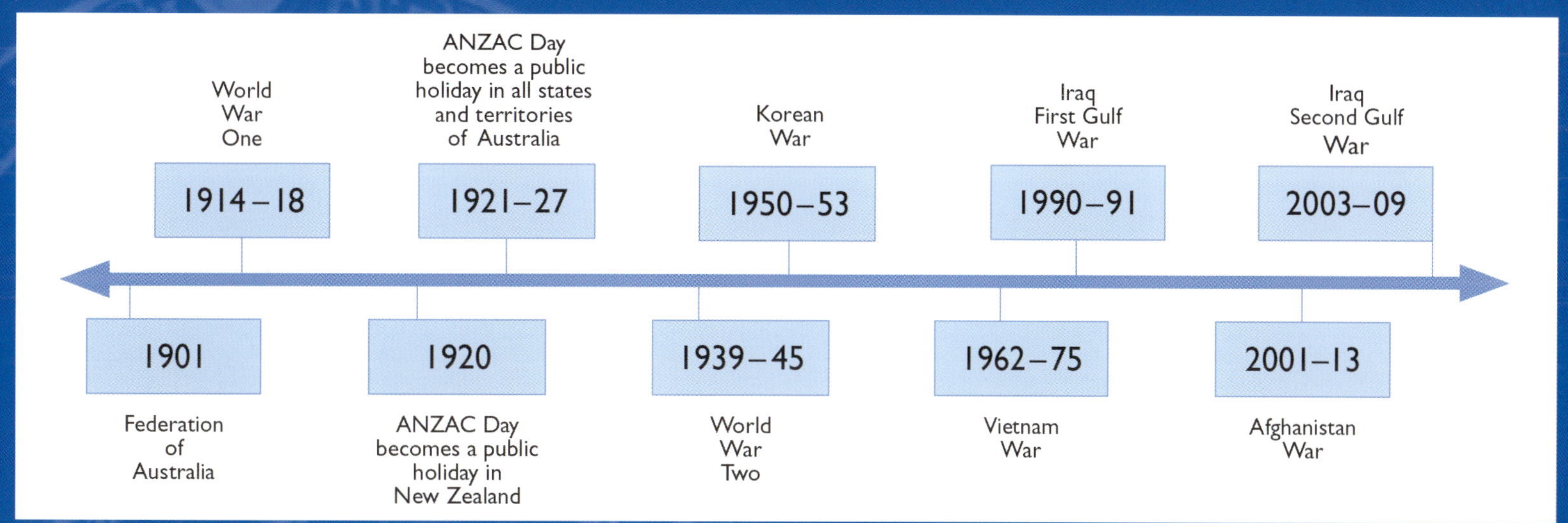

They say, 'You must be so proud',

'to have a Daddy so brave.
He served his country
to make the world a safer place
and didn't die in vain.'

War is always a **tragedy**. There are really no winners. Each group has their own memorials, stories and perspectives. Many groups and countries who have previously engaged in war are now friends. At ANZAC Cove, there is part of Kemal Atatürk's famous speech transcribed on the memorial that reflects this change in attitude.

At Gallipoli, there is now a statue of the last survivor from the Turkish Army who fought at ANZAC Cove, holding the hand of his granddaughter. In this region, rosemary grows naturally in many places and has long been associated with remembering this time. Turkish visitors place sprigs of the fresh rosemary into the granddaughter's hands. Australians and New Zealanders often wear a sprig of rosemary on ANZAC Day as a **symbol of remembrance**.

'Those heroes that shed their blood and lost their lives … you are now lying in soil of a friendly country. Therefore rest in peace. There is no difference between the **Johnnies** and the **Mehmets** to us where they lie side-by-side here in this country of ours … You, the mothers, who sent their sons from far-away countries, wipe away your tears: your sons are now lying in our bosom and are in peace. After having lost their lives on this land they have become our sons as well.'

Kemal Atatürk, 1934 (Commander of the 9th Division during the Gallipoli campaign and then President of the Turkish Republic 1924–1938).

Turkish Memorial, Gallipoli

I don't know about that.

I'd rather have my Dad,
right beside me right now,
right beside me every day.

The soldiers who go to war are someone's brother or sister, mum or dad, son or daughter and, of course, they have a lot of friends and relations too. So many people in our communities are affected when a soldier is killed or comes home with **physical or mental injuries.**

Do you know of anyone who has been affected by war?

What might you say to someone who is affected by war?

How could you show them you care?

I would rather have my Dad,

teach me to ride my bike,
read and play with me and
see me get my school awards.

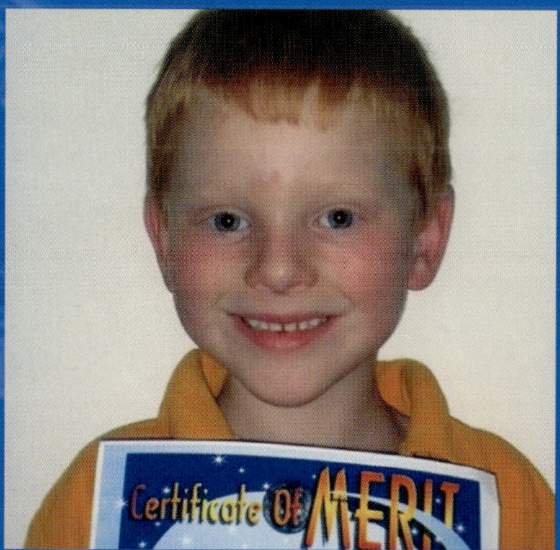

and I would rather have him here ...

to share his things with me,
to take me to the beach,
and to go for a walk in the bush.

Mum says, ‘Come on Liam’.

The day’s not over yet, we’re off to have breakfast at the **Ex-Services Club**.

The Returned and Services League (RSL) assists veteran soldiers. Other organisations have special roles too, like Legacy and Soldier On. They often sell pins, badges, bears and other merchandise to raise money for the work they do.

Do you or your family know about any of these charities?

Have you or your family ever supported one of these charities?

Then we head off to the march,

and what an amazing sight —
the colours, the flags, the cars
and the medals shining bright.

There are **service men and women,**

cadets, police and school children.
A **pipe band, a marching band** and the crowd who points, waves and smiles.

The march is long,

then at the park there are **speeches**. My Dad's name is said again and the **wreath laying** begins.

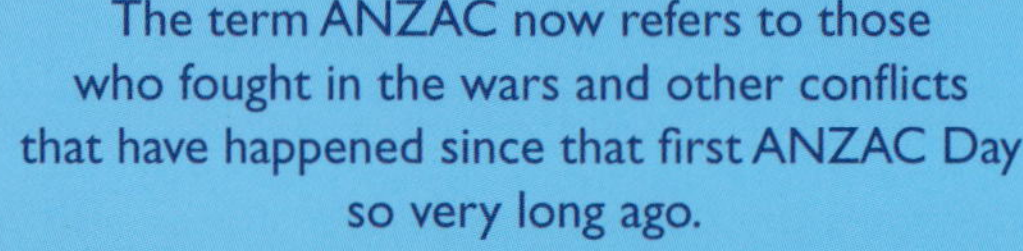

The term ANZAC now refers to those who fought in the wars and other conflicts that have happened since that first ANZAC Day so very long ago.

After that there are *more* photos

and they want Mum to make me smile.
But my smiles have all gone,
it's raining and I just want to go home.

Have you ever marched on ANZAC Day?

Which community groups, services and schools did you see march that day?

What else did you see?

ANZAC marches and services can be long. We remember not only the original ANZACs but all who have served in times of war. In some towns and cities, community groups, school children and family members of service men and women, will join the march out of respect for all who have served.

... but tell me again, why do I wear Dad's medals?

Many Australian and New Zealand soldiers have died in foreign countries. Some were brought home to be buried on home soil. Most have a grave where they died overseas. We do not know where some of our service men and women are buried but we still remember them all the same. We remember because these men and women went to war to make our world a safer and fairer place. The tombs of the Unknown Soldier and Unknown Warrior are symbols of the respect and remembrance that Australia and New Zealand hold for those who have served their country but who have not returned home.

The Tomb of the Unknown Warrior New Zealand, National War Memorial, Wellington

Villers Bretonneux Cemetery, France

The Tomb of the Unknown Soldier, Hall of Remembrance, Australian War Memorial, Canberra

Again they say, 'You must be so proud ...'

'to have a Daddy so brave.'
But sometimes I am brave too
and so is my Mum.

How are Liam and his Mum brave?

Events and circumstances are often out of our control. Being good does not mean good things will always happen. The one thing people can control is their attitude. No matter what happens to us and our families, we can be brave by making the most of our lives and helping others.

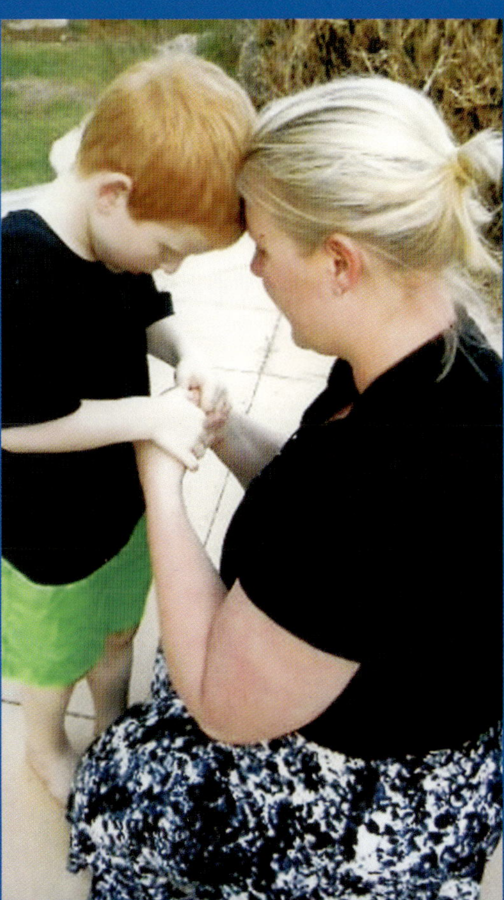

I say, 'I want Dad to come back.'

I feel sad when I see kids with their dads at the park and at school.

Soldiers who do return from war to their homes are usually changed in many ways. They have seen and experienced events that have shocked and saddened them. These events are not easily forgotten. At times they need extra support. Those who are injured, mentally and physically, often require ongoing **treatment**. Charities such as Soldier On and other veteran organisations assist this **rehabilitation** with many **medical and associated health professionals**.

Mum hugs me and sniffs,

sighs and frowns. She says,
'No, he can't come back from where he is',
and I can see she is trying not to cry.

' ... so tell me again, why do I wear Dad's medals?'

When somebody we love and we need dies, we still want to feel close to that person. Sometimes having their special things makes us feel closer to them. Doing something that they would have done, if they were here, can make us less sad. Often special dates are remembered like their birthdays or the **anniversary** of the day they died.

What do you think Liam does to remember his Dad?

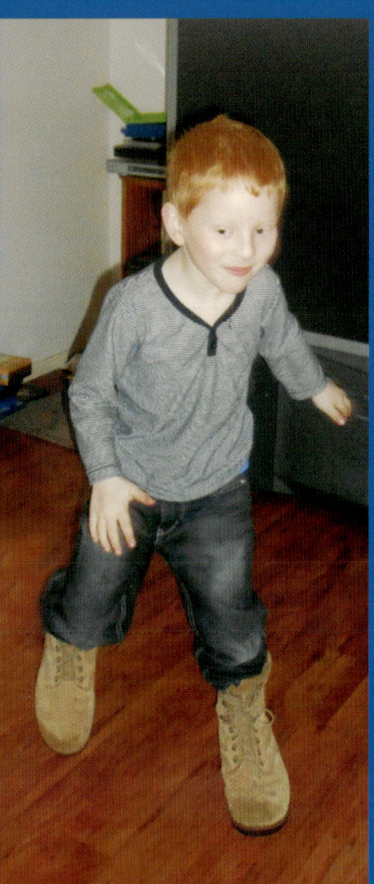

I know my Dad was killed

when I was a little baby,
in a far away place,
in a far away war.

My Dad was a soldier

and Mum says 'He was more than that! He was a Dad, a husband, a friend, a son, and a man who enjoyed his work.'

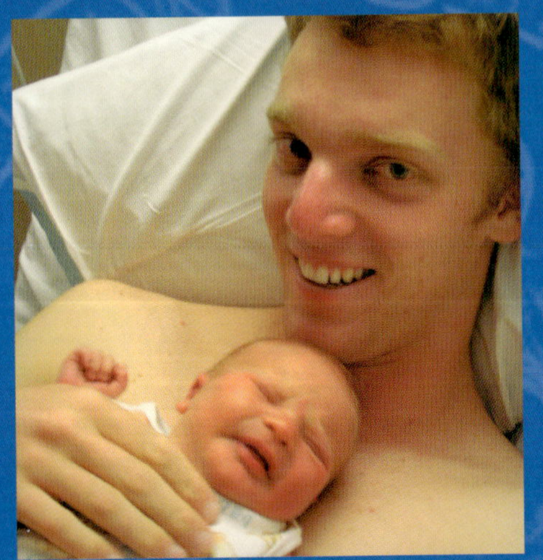

And then next time someone asks,

'So why do you wear your Dad's medals?'

On ANZAC Day, marchers wear their medals for lots of reasons:

- as a sign of respect for their mates who didn't come back,
- as a mark of pride for their **achievements**,
- as a symbol of what they fought for — a **free nation**,
- in acknowledgement of all who have served in the past, and
- in memory of those who used to march.

Glossary

Acknowledgement — give credit to.
Acronym — an abbreviation formed by creating a single word from the first letters of words in a word group or phrase, e.g. ADF (Australian Defence Force), ANZAC (Australian and New Zealand Army Corp).
Active service — military duties undertaken by men and women in the ADF (army, navy, airforce) during operations, often overseas.
Allied forces — countries that join forces to fight together.
Anniversary — a day we remember every year because it falls on the same day as a past event that is still important to us.
Army Corp — a large group of ADF men and women who share the same task or purpose.
Attitude — a feeling or thought we choose to have that shapes our reactions to different situations and events.
Border protection — all countries are defined by borders. Countries use border protection to ensure that people and/or supplies do not enter without permission.
Bugle — A brass instrument with no valves (buttons) making it good for battle because it needs little servicing. Having no valves means that the player must be skillful in making each note by adjusting their lips and air pressure. It also means it has a limited number of notes it can play.
Campaign — a large and long important military operation that has a particular goal and requires planning, often as part of a longer operation.
Catafalque party (cat-a-falk) — a group of soldiers who represent a guard for the coffin of a soldier (originally from a French and Italian word meaning alongside or scaffolding [supporting]).
Celebration — a gathering to mark a special and happy occasion, for example, a graduation.
Charity — a not-for-profit organisation formed to assist people or animals in need.
Coffin — a box, normally made of wood, that is used to bury a body,
Commemoration — a ceremony to mark the anniversary of a significant event in our history.
Community — a group of people who share common bonds, for example because they live in the same area, work in the same place or have shared interests.
Comrade — friend or colleague.

Conflict — a situation in which there is strong disagreement or a dispute that can lead to war, for example, in a country where there is fighting between the government and some of its citizens.

Ex-services club — These clubs were originally set up as places for ex-service personnel to meet, socialise and be supported in many ways. They were set up after World War Two but have changed in their approach to business and the community they serve.

Federation — the process in which the six separate colonial governments on the Australian continent prior to 1901 combined to form one nation in 1901.

Foreign countries — a country which is not your own and where you are not a citizen. (Because Australia and New Zealand are both islands foreign countries are often referred to as overseas.)

Free nation — a country whose people are able to vote to choose their own government.

Gallantry — courageous or brave behaviour, especially during military operations.

Injury — damage experienced by soldiers as a result of taking part in a conflict or war; it can be both physical (e.g. loss of an arm or leg) or mental (e.g. depression).

Johnnie — the name used by Kemal Atatürk for soldiers from countries fighting against Turkey during World War One.

Kemal Atatürk — Commander in 1915 of the Turkish army at Gallipoli and later in 1923 was the first president of the Turkish Republic.

Marches — formal meetings of people with common beliefs or to commemorate or celebrate a particular event or day.

Marching band — a band who plays in marches, normally with instruments suited for marching. They help to keep the marchers in time and add to the atmosphere for the crowds.

Medical and associated health professionals — doctors, nurses, physiotherapists, dentists, counsellors, surgeons etc.

Mehmet — the name used by Kemal Atatürk for Turkish soldiers.

Memorial/monument — a man-made structure in a public area to remember people or an event, e.g. wars, the names of ADF personnel.

Merchandise — goods and products for sale, e.g. goods sold by a charity to raise money and build awareness of the charity and its work.

Morning services — a service that is held to commemorate those who have served our country. These usually occur after the morning march on ANZAC Day.

Ode — a short three-part poem or verse recited in order to praise and honour one or more individuals, e.g. to remember and honour those who died during conflicts and wars.

Peacekeeping mission — a group of military personnel, often from different countries, whose job is to help keep or make possible peace between two warring groups.

Perspective — a point of view, which may be different from another person's point of view.

Pipe band — a band that features the bagpipes and often drums. Bagpipes are an ideal outdoor instrument and are often added to marches for their cultural and historic significance. In ancient times they were used to stir the emotions of soldiers before they set off to battle. In services and marches they often stir deep emotions.

Public holiday — a special holiday set aside in the calendar of the country by the government.
Rations — a fixed and limited amount of food, often pre-prepared, provided to each person during a food shortage, conflict or war.
Rehabilitation — treatment (e.g. exercises and special activities) to assist people (e.g. ADF personnel) to return to normal life after physical or mental injury.
Replica — a copy of an item that might be exactly the same, or to a different scale, e.g. medals worn by ADF personnel that are sometimes recreated in miniatures for Defence families.
Rolls of honour — a list of names of those who died in wars, often inscribed on boards and placed in significant local buildings or on memorials.
Service men and women/service personnel — men and women who work for the army, navy or airforce of their country.
Speeches — formal talks by invited guests at the services.
Seriously early — colloquial expression meaning very, very early.
Surveillance — keep under observation, the movement, activities and behaviour of people in order to make effective decisions to maintain or achieve peace.
Symbol — an object, word or image that stands for a feeling, idea, events or group of people (e.g. on ANZAC day rosemary stands for all who died).
Tomb — a place for burying the dead.
Tragedy — a deeply sad event or series of events that causes suffering and/or death.
Traumatically affected — sometimes people see or are involved in a tragedy and this deeply affects them for a long time.
Unknown soldier/warrior — a soldier or warrior killed in war who has never been found or identified. In Australia and New Zealand the tomb of the unknown soldier/warrior is a national memorial and a symbol for all soldiers who have not been found.
Veteran — a person who has experience in a particular occupation, for example, defence personnel who have completed service with the ADF.
Volunteers — a person who performs a service without being paid. It can also mean someone who has nominated themself to serve their country without being asked.
War — an extended and usually very violent and disruptive conflict within or between countries.
War zone — an area during active conflict where only service personnel are supposed to be. Civilians are not allowed to enter because it is dangerous.
Wreath — a ring of flowers and leaves placed on monuments and memorials, for example, to remember and honour those who have died in wars.

What the literature and research says

By Marg Baber

This book explores themes identified by Marg Baber in a doctoral study undertaken at the University of New England entitled 'Young Children's Understanding and Experiences of Deployment within an Australian Defence Force Family'. The themes are acculturation, narrative and ritual, protective factors and resilience.

Acculturation

Acculturation is defined as the changes that occur within individuals or groups of people when they mix with another culture (Burton, Westen and Kowalski, 2012). A culture is shared behaviour or rules that a group of people exhibit in order to function effectively as they communicate and work together (Lawrence, Brooker and Goodnow, 2012). Individuals and groups undergoing acculturation take on characteristics of the new culture, while retaining only certain aspects of their own culture. The degree to which people become acculturated depends on many factors, including their age and circumstances, how dominant they perceive the new culture to be, and the pressure they feel to keep their own culture in relation to the pressures placed on them by the new culture. In Australia, the culture of Australian Defence Force (ADF) families can often be quite tight, which means, as Burton, *et al* (2012) outline, that ADF members and their families are encouraged or 'expected to adhere to cultural norms and expectations' (p19), in order to strengthen their community. How this is achieved is often through the use of narrative and ritual.

Narrative and ritual

Children construct an understanding of their world through their experiences and their culture (Gonzalez-Mena and Widmeyer Eyer, 1997). Culture shapes parental ideals about children's behaviour as well as the traits, aptitudes and learning of the child (Saggers and Sims, 2005). For example, from within his ADF family and the broader ADF community, Liam learns the values and expectations of his community through ADF rituals, commemorations, celebrations and narratives. Membership of this close community helps build resilience in ADF families because of the protective factors it affords.

Protective factors

In many ways the ADF culture is a supportive one, in which families experiencing family stress as a result of deployment, training and, in Liam's case, grief, rely on each other for emotional and physical support. Additional assistance is offered to ADF families by organisations such as Legacy and the Returned and Services League (RSL). On the other hand, returned service personnel strongly resist reaching out for help for themselves and their family members when it comes to mental health issues for fear of severely diminishing their chances of re-deployment or career advancement (Brown, 2014; Siebler, 2009).

The stoic military family is an iconic ideal that many ADF families emulate in their behaviour and beliefs (Siebler, 2009). Reaching out for support can, therefore, be interpreted as a lack of stoicism and as non-military behaviour. The stigma associated with seeking help for mental health problems also occurs within the broader community (Arthur, Beecher, Death, Dockett and Farmer, 2008). For some families, such as the family in this book, the relationship with the ADF is multi-generational, which brings with it added expectations, both familial and cultural (Vickers, 2013), about how ADF support systems work. These extended family relationships can be disrupted by geographic and social isolation when families are deployed to distant locations where they are faced with initiating and nurturing new relationships (Arthur et al., 2008). Isolation is also a factor when an ADF member passes away, as happened to the family featured in this book. Those left behind feel as if they are teetering between belonging to the ADF and being separated from it. Ideally, to assist with building resilience, this family should be able to access support from both the ADF and the general community.

Resilience

Nurturing resilience in families, individuals and communities during periods of high stress can be achieved through social support across a range of contexts and levels (Burton et al., 2012), including through loving and supportive relationships. These supports can shift the person's view of both the stressful situation itself and their ability to cope with it. Educators are often a vital link between support services and families (Arthur, Beecher, Death, Docket, & Farmer, 2012). For many, like Liam's family, knowing support is available, even if they do not access it formally, can be reassuring (Burton et al., 2012).

Teaching History in Primary Schools

By Madeline Fussell and Kim Porter

Australian and New Zealand curriculum documents emphasise that students in primary school must develop the skills and knowledge they need to be active and informed 21st century citizens. Assisting students to understand the cause and effect of past events and the significance of these events in our lives today helps them to reflect on and form values that will impact and inspire their future involvement in the community (Australian Curriculum and Reporting Authority, 2011; Ministry of Education New Zealand, 2014). This book enables students to explore the ANZAC tradition, both in terms of how it has changed over the years and how support for the commemoration of ANZAC continues to increase with time. The exploration of change and continuity in relation to the ANZAC tradition can be achieved through programming that combines narrative with an inquiry approach.

Narrative

Narrative has been identified as one of the six dimensions of quality teaching (NSW Department of Education and Training, 2003). Narrative is described in contemporary curriculum documents as a powerful strategy for assisting students to understand that historical events can be interpreted from many different perspectives.

When narrative is used in the teaching of history in primary school, students come to understand the significance of historical events and to feel a connection with the people who experienced those events, including events the students, hopefully, will never have to experience themselves. In this book the use of a child's narrative not only gives students insight into the significance of a tradition with its origin in historical events, but also enables a deeper engagement and connection with those for whom this tradition remains alive as students empathise with Liam's longing for his father.

The narrative told in this book can also be used to assist secondary students to develop historical empathy (Taylor, 2012; Reynolds, 2012) at many levels; for example, as a stimulus to initiate teaching and learning activities that involve critical thinking. A narrative such as this can also be used in the wider community to build knowledge and understanding of the significance of ANZAC Day in both Australia and New Zealand.

Inquiry

The inquiry approach advocated in contemporary curriculum documents should always commence with a question such as the one which initiates the narrative in this book: 'Why do I wear dad's medals?'. A question such as this provides students with a clear direction for undertaking their inquiry. With teacher guidance, they can use the question to process and personalise the information they gather.

In our research, inquiry-based teaching strategies were used to help students in multi-age classrooms in small schools to explore ANZAC traditions. This study revealed two important findings. First, it showed that primary school children could relate to and develop deep learning in relation to this subject matter when the learning built on the children's prior knowledge and experience using hands-on activities, and when narrative was used both to engage and to explain unfamiliar experiences and events. Second, the study revealed that despite an abundance of information about ANZAC traditions, very little of this information is available in narrative form suitable for younger children and an inquiry-based approach. Moreover, to the best of our knowledge, there are no early childhood resources that highlight how our current service men and women, and their families, understand and experience ANZAC traditions. This book, we hope, will help to fill this gap by not only answering Liam's probing and poignant question but also by helping children who have no connection with the personal cost of war build understanding and empathy for those whom war has, and still does, affect.

Teaching within the early childhood classroom

By Marg Baber

The ANZAC tradition is an integral part of the Australian and New Zealand culture and it is important that our young children understand the meanings underpinning this tradition. This is recognised in both the Australian Early Years Learning Framework (DEEWR, 2009) and National Quality Framework (ACECQA, 2012) and New Zealand's Te Whāriki (Ministry of Education, 1996) which all emphasise working with young children to ensure they respect diversity, understand the richness of our traditions and connect with family and community. Exploring the answers to Liam's question 'Why do I wear Dad's medals?' promotes children's respect for diverse perspectives (DEEWR, 2009) by providing them with resources that broaden their own perspectives. Including community and cultural events within early childhood programs contributes to children's learning and development. It also helps to build their sense of identity and belonging within their community according to the National Quality Framework (ACECQA, 2012). The tag line questions throughout the text invite educators to 'support the investigation of ideas, complex concepts and thinking, reasoning and hypothesising' (DEEWR, 2009, p. 35) and through this reasoning children may build their own theories to make sense of the world (New Zealand Ministry of Education, 1996).

Image reference list

ANZAC Cove, vintage car, New Zealand flag: Shutterstock.
Catafalque soldier and Tomb of the Unknown Warrior service: Flikr — New Zealand Defence Force <https://farm8.staticflickr.com/7262/7444468648_c0256c6687.jpg>.
Catafalque party, wreath laying at service, The Armidale School used with kind permission.
Drummers, female veteran with son, Darrel Whan, used with kind permission from *The Armidale Express*.
Flag raising, female veteran, piper, bugler, veteran on scooter, school group marching, police, pipe band marching, school children with floral tribute, school children with wreath, Darrel Whan, used with kind permission.
Front cover photo, supplied by the NSW RSL.
Memorial of Turkish soldier, Turkish tour guide, mother ironing, clothes on bed, putting on shirt, putting on trousers, march with Army and Navy soldiers, medals, Turkish grandfather and grandchild, Attatürk's speech memorial, climbing tree, riding bike, reading, playing in cubby house, playing with toys, looking at compass, looking at bookcase, breakfast at Ex-Services club, Legacy bears, Legacy volunteer, Wandering Warriors SAS veterans, Villers Bretonneux Cemetery headstone and cemetery, Tomb of Unknown Soldier, mother and child sad, mother and child happy, child on climbing web, child looking at parents' portrait, child with boots sequence, Madeline Fussell.
Newspaper article with poppies and rosemary (*Weekend Australian*, 26–7 April 2014), children with flags, Kim Porter
Tomb of Unknown Warrior, New Zealand, Flikr — New Zealand Defence Force <https://farm6.staticflickr.com/5310/5651943392_79fb6454fc.jpg>.
All other photos supplied by defence families and organisations.

Reference list

Arthur L, Beecher B, Death E, Dockett S and Farmer S (2008) *Programming and planning in early childhood settings*. (4th edn). South Melbourne, Nelson Australia Pty Limited.

Arthur L, Beecher B, Death E, Docket S and Farmer S (2012). *Programming and Planing in Early Childhood Settings*. South Melbourne: Cengage Learning Australia Pty Limited.

Australian Children's Education and Care Quality Authority. (2011). Guide to the National Quality Standard. Canberra, ACT: Australian Children's Education and Care Quality Authority. Canberra, ACT, Australia: Australian Children's Education and Care Quality Authority Retrieved from <http://acecqa.gov.au/storage/3-Guide to the National Quality Standard FINAL.pdf>.

Australian Curriculum and Reporting Authority (2011), 'History (Foundation to Year 10)'. Retrieved from <http://www.acara.edu.au/verve/_resources/Information_Sheet_History_2011.pdf#search=history>.

Brown R (Producer) (2014, 23.4.14), 'Australian Defence Force veterans detail growing scourge of post-traumatic stress disorder', ABC News [Article], Retrieved from <http://www.abc.net.au/news/2014-04-23/rising-ptsd-compensation-figures-in-adf-only-the-start/5404778>.

Burton L, Westen D and Kowalski R (2012) *Psychology* (3rd Australian and New Zealand edn), Milton, QLD, Australia: John Wiley & Sons Australia Ltd.

DEEWR. (2009). *Early Years Learning Framework*. Canberra, ACT, Australia: Australian Government.

Gonzalez-Mena J and Widmeyer Eyer D (1997) Infants, toddlers and caregivers (4th edn), Mountain View, CA, Mayfield Publishing Company.

Hoepper B (2014) 'History in the Australian curriculum', in R Gilbert and B Hoepper (Eds), *Teaching humanities and social sciences. History, geography, economics & citizenship in the Australian curriculum* (pp 176–95), South Melbourne, Australia, Cengage Learning.

Lawrence J, Brooker A and Goodnow J (2012) 'Ethnicity: Finding a cultural home in Australia', in J Bowes, R Grace and K Hodge (Eds), *Children, families and communities: Contexts and Consequences* (4th edn), South Melbourne, Oxford University Press.

Ministry of Education (New Zealand) (1996). *Te Whariki: Early Childhood Curriculum*. Wellington, New Zealand: Learning Media.

Ministry of Education (New Zealand) (2014) *The New Zealand Curriculum Online*, 'Social Sciences', Retrieved from <http://nzcurriculum.tki.org.nz/The-New-Zealand-Curriculum/Learning-areas/Social-sciences>.

NSW Department of Education and Training Professional Support and Curriculum Directorate (2003), *Quality teaching in NSW public schools*, Sydney, State of NSW Department of Education and Training Professional Support and Curriculum Directorate (In audiovisual kit).

Newmann F and Associates (1996) *Authentic Achievement: Restructuring Schools for Intellectual Quality,* San Francisco, Jossey-Bass.

Queensland Department of Education, Training and Employment (2014) 'Productive pedagogies', retrieved from, <http://education.qld.gov.au/staff/learning/diversity/teaching/teaching.html>.

Reynolds R (2012) *Teaching history, geography & SOSE in the primary school*, 2nd edn, South Melbourne, Oxford University Press.

Saggers S and Sims M (2005) 'Diversity: Beyond the nuclear family', in M Poole (Ed), *Family: Changing families, changing times.* Sydney, Allen & Unwin.

Siebler P (2009) 'Military people won't ask for help: Experiences of deployment of Australian Defence Force personnel, their families and implications for social work' (Doctor of Philosophy), Monash University.

Taylor T (2012) 'Progression in understanding in history', in T Taylor, C Fahey, J Kriewaldt and D Boon (Eds), *Place and time. Explorations in teaching geography and history* (pp 191–215). Sydney, Pearson Australia.

Vickers M (2013) 'Curriculum', in R Connell, A Welch, M Vickers, D Foley, N Bagnall, D Hayes, H Proctor, A Spiprakash and C Campbell (Eds), *Education, change and society* (3rd edn). South Melbourne, Oxford University Press.

Links for extension activities and teaching programs

For extension activities and teaching programs suitable for parents and teachers that have been written by Madeline Fussell, Kim Porter and Susan Feez and edited by Marg Baber, please go to www.pademelonpress.com.au and search for the page for Liam's Story.

About the authors and editors

Marg Baber is a lecturer and researcher in Early Childhood education at the University of New England. She has qualifications and professional experience in Early Childhood, creative arts education and ESL. In both her current and previous work roles, her passion in education has always been in supporting families to help them do the best job they can through authentic community and education partnerships. As a part of this project, Marg has had the privilege to meet with some defence families and discuss many of the issues they face. Marg hopes this book and others in the planning will help children, parents and educators have a starting point to discuss these issues further. She is researching 'Young Children's Understanding and Experiences within an Australian Defence Force Family'. Marg would like to dedicate this book to Uncle Bruce who spins the best yarns in the family (and Aunty Joan who still laughs at them all). He served in Vietnam.

Madeline Fussell was the person contacted by the family reflected in this book and thus this project has held special meaning for her. As a primary trained and early childhood educator, Madeline has 28 years teaching experience , the most recent as a lecturer in Social Sciences at the University of New England teaching pre-service primary teachers. Teaching about implementing the Australian history curriculum, Madeline identified a clear lack of suitable resources for early years and primary aged students. Madeline's own childhood with a father who battled PTSD and her learning through her own two sons', and their friends', military careers has been a driving force to see development of further community understanding of veterans' needs, and those of their families.

Kim Porter is a lecturer in Social Science teaching (primary education) at the University of New England. She brings 26 years of primary teaching expertise to this book, including her knowledge and competence in specialised areas such as Reading Recovery and how to engage reluctant readers. Kim's commitment to the book was driven through a desire to see a quality text that would appeal to, and engage, students across the early and primary years. The meaningfulness of ANZAC Day took on another dimension for Kim when she supported a close friend through the loss of her son in a military conflict. Kim hopes that Liam's personal story will add meaning for some, and significance for all Australian and New Zealand citizens.

Dr Susan Feez is a senior lecturer in the School of Education, University of New England. She teaches and researches in the fields of languages and literacies education, English as an additional language and educational linguistics. She also has qualifications and expertise in Montessori early childhood and primary education. Susan is an experienced classroom teacher and has taught in early childhood, primary and junior secondary school, as well as in adult education. She has collaborated on a series of recent education publications that reflect her interest in fast tracking educational innovation derived from research into classrooms.

Acknowledgments

The authors would like to acknowledge the special family who asked for this book to be created and thus highlighted the glaring need for age-appropriate Australian books and for community understanding of veteran families. Thanks must also go to the Defence families and relatives who have made themselves available for this project, giving their time, photographs, generosity and honesty. Many thanks also to Black Mountain and Niangala Public schools, and their enthusiastic teachers and students, who combined with us in an action research project to explore teaching strategies for creating a unit of work on the ANZAC story that would be suitable for primary aged students. Huge thanks to the families, organisations and friends who also contributed their time, photos and memories to make this book a reality. A special thanks to Di for her administrative support and Beth Rogers for her grammatical advice.

The publishers wish to thank the following organisations for their support of *Liam's Story*.

RSL (NSW)

RSA (NZ)

Legacy

Defence Care

Soldier On

www.soldieron.org.au

Soldier On's mission is to achieve the best re-integrated generation of service men and service women in Australia's history. Through our programs, we work to:

- **Enhance** the recovery of Australia's wounded by investing in rehabilitative equipment and programs;
- **Connect** them with their families and broader communities through specific campaigns, events and programs;
- **Inspire** these men and women to seek help for their own struggles following service by sharing the stories of those we support; and
- **Empower** them to become productive and successful members of their community through education and employment.